Time for English
Workbook 3

Geraldine Sweeney and Gabrielle Pritchard

Series consultant:
Dr Maha El Said
Lecturer
English Department, Faculty of Arts
Cairo University

MACMILLAN

Macmillan Education
Between Towns Road, Oxford OX4 3PP
A division of Macmillan Publishers Limited
Companies and representatives throughout the world

www.macmillan-africa.com
www.macmillan-caribbean.com

ISBN-13: 978-0-333-68540-2

Typeset by A Tek-Art,
Illustrated by A Tek-Art
Cover design by Wheeler and Porter

Printed by Zamzam Presses, Egypt

2010   2009   2008   2007
10   9

All about me

1 Draw, colour and write about yourself.

I'm _12_ years old.

I'm _tall_ . (tall/short)

I have got _long_
hair. (long/short)

I have got _curly_
hair. (straight/curly)

I have got _brown_
eyes. (blue/green/brown)

2 Read and write answers to the questions. (Yes, I do./No, I don't.)

A Do you like pizza? _Yes, I do_

B Do you like cats?  _No, I don't_

C Do you like football? _No, I don't_

D Do you like computers? _Yes, I do_

E Do you like orange juice? _Yes, I do_

F Do you like tea? _Yes, I do_

3 Draw your house and fill the gaps.

shopping centre
mosque
book shop
airport
river
petrol station
pharmacy
bus station
cinema
swimming pool
supermarket
sports centre
school

This is my house. I live near the *bus stop*

My telephone number is   03 89 42 09 25

4 Read and tick.

In my house there's a . . .

A	⚽	football ☐	B	🚲	bike ☑		
C	🐱	cat ☐	D	💻	computer ☑		
E	📻	radio ☑	F	📺	TV ☑		
G	🍳	cooker ☑	H	🧊	fridge ☑		
I	🎹	piano ☐	J	🪑	table ☑		
K	🕐	clock ☑	L	🪜	ladder ☐		

5 Read and answer the questions. (Yes, I can./No, I can't.)

A   Can you ride a bike? _Yes, I can_

B   Can you play the piano? _No, I can't_

C   Can you run? _Yes, I can_

D   Can you catch a ball? _Yes, I can_

E   Can you use a computer? _Yes, I can_

F   Can you sing? _Yes, I can_

G   Can you swim? _No, I can't_

6 Draw and write.

I can ride a bike.   I can _sing_ .

At the football ground

● 1 Circle the mistakes. Look at your Pupil's Book, page 4.

A

My name is Jack. I'm 8 years old. I've got 2 brothers, Karim and Alex, and a sister, Suzy. I live near the airport.

B

My name is Suzy. I'm 8 years old. I live near the airport. I've got 2 brothers, Dina and Amira.

Correct the false sentences.

_____

_____

_____

_____

● 2 Time to answer the questions about yourself.

A What's your name? _My name is Sabine_

B How old are you? _I have 12 years old_

C Have you got any brothers and sisters? _I have 2 sisters, Sajaa and siraa, I have 1 brother, Mohammed._

D Where do you live? _I live near the bus stop_

● 3 Read and complete. Look at Pupil's Book page 5.

A My father is a _____ .

B My __Mo_____ is a teacher.

C My Uncle Reda is a _____ .

D My Aunt Zeinab is a _____ .

E My _____ , Ali, is a policeman.

F My sister, Dina, is a _____ .

4 Read and write: Yes, we have. or No, we haven't.

A Have we got any aubergines? _Yes, we have_ +

B Have we got any eggs? _No, we haven't_

C Have we got any tomatoes? _Yes, we have_

D Have we got any oranges? _No, we haven't_

Now answer these questions:

E How many potatoes have we got? **We've got 5 potatoes.**

F How many chillies have we got? _We've got 4 chillies_

G How many olives have we got? _We've got 3 olives_

H How many bananas have we got? _We've got 2 bananas_

5 Time to read and complete.

A Would you like some **tea**, Amira?   Yes, please.

B Would you like some _bread_, Amira?   Yes, _please_.

C Would you like _some_ yoghurt?   No, _thank you_!

thank you	
please	
some	
tea ✔	
bread	

6 Choose and write, then answer.

A

I'm swimming.
I'm sleeping

I'm swimming.

B

I'm sleeping.
I'm jumping

I'm sleeping

C

I'm sweeping.
I'm sleeping

I'm sweepin

D

What are you doing, Jack?

Jack's ridding

E

What are you doing, Amira?

Amira's playing tennes

7 Time to write sentences.

A

Mahmoud/mosque

Mahmoud is going to the mosque.

B

Jack/shop

Jack is going to te shop

C

Amira/park

Amira is going to the park

D
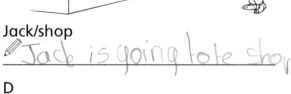

Suzy/school

Suzy is going to to school

Unit 2 Meeting people

1 Match the questions and answers.

A
What's his name?

His family name is Ahmed. **A**

His family name is Saeed.

B
What's her name?

His first name is Amin.

Her family name is Kureishi.

C
What's his name?

Her first name is Dalia.

His first name is Farid.

2 Time to read and complete.

A

YOUSSEF HASSAN

His family name is ___Hassan___
His first name ___youssef___

B

SUZY GREENWOOD

Her family name is ___Greenwood___
Her ___First name is Suzy___

C

MUNIR HASSAN

His family name is Munir
His first name is Hassan

D

MARY HARDING

Her family name is Mary
Her first name is Harding

Unit 2 9

3 Time to complete the sums.

10 + 3 = _thirteen_   fifteen + three = _eighteen_

5 + 1 = _six_   twelve + three = _fifteen_

6 + 6 = _twelve_   eight + six = _forteen_

9 + 10 = _nineteen_   twelve + four = _sixteen_

4 Circle the mistakes and write the true sentences.

A

B

C

Magda Khalil
20 Al Manfaluti Street

Osman Bakri
14 Ibn Battuta Road

Nadia Habib
12 Al Medina Avenue

A Her name is Magda Khalil. Her address is 12 Al Manfaluti Road.

Her name is Magda Khalil. Her address is 8 Al Manfalut S

B His name is Osman Bakri. His address is 14 Ibn Battuta Avenue.

His name is Osman Bakri. His address is 14 Ibn Battuta Road

C Her name is Nadia Hussein. Her address is 12 Al Aqsa Avenue.

Her name is Nadia Hussein. Her address is 12 Al Medina Avenue

5 Time to read the card and fill the gaps.

First name: __Abbas__

Family name: __Rashid__

Address: __116 Nasser Street__

Telephone number: __57839__

His first name is _Abbas_ . His family name is _Rashid_ . His address is _116 Nasser street_ and his telephone number is _57839_.

Now complete this card for your friend.

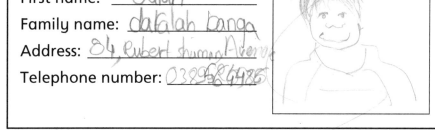

First name: _Gulah_

Family name: _dakalah banga_

Address: _84, rubert shuman Avenue_

Telephone number: _0389586485_

Her first name is Gulah. Her family name is dakalah banga. His adrex is 84, Avenue rubert shuman and Her telephone number is 0389586485

6 Put your family's names in alphabetical order.

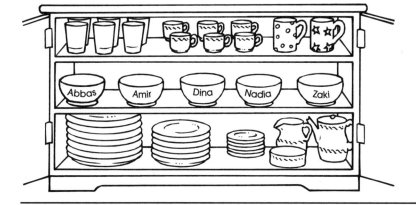

Abdel Halim
Mohammed-riyad
Rasha
Sajoa
Sakina
Siraa

Mother's Day

● **1 Read and write this or that.**

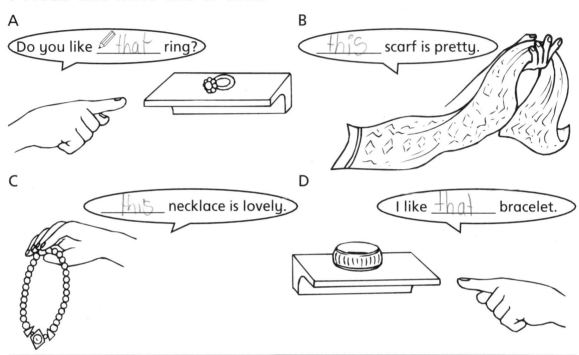

A

Do you like *that* ring?

B

this scarf is pretty.

C

this necklace is lovely.

D

I like *that* bracelet.

● **2 Time to read and complete.**

lovely   these   like   pretty   these   those

Karim: Do you like _____these_____ rings?

Amira: Yes, they're _____lovely_____, but look at _____those_____ handbags.

Karim: Yes, they're very nice. But do you _____like_____ these earrings?

Amira: They're OK, but _____these_____ bracelets are _____pretty_____.

3 Time to draw and write.

What's that in English?

It's a _pen_.

Tell your friend to draw 6 things in your Workbook. Write the names in English.

1 _Iure = book_ 2 _____ 3 _____

4 _____ 5 _____ 6 _____

4 Read, draw and colour.

A

Do you like this black handbag?

B

These red earrings are pretty.

C

I don't like that yellow scarf.

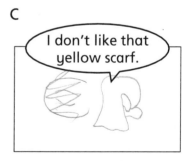

D

Those blue necklaces are very nice.

E

Look at these rings! They're lovely!

5 Read and write.

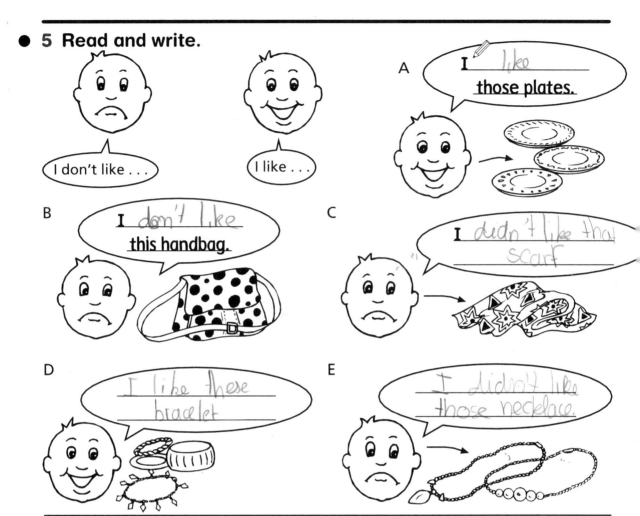

I don't like . . .

I like . . .

A I ___like___ those plates.

B I ___don't like___ this handbag.

C I ___didn't like that scarf___

D ___I like these bracelet___

E ___I didn't like those necklace.___

6 Time to write the rhyme.

book   rice   rings   bike

A This ___rice___ is nice!

B Look at this ___book___ !

C These ___rings___ are pretty things!

D I like that ___bike___ !

Unit 4 Revision

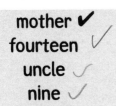

1 Time to sort and write.

mother ✔	aunt	brother	sister	cousin
fourteen ✓	doctor	policeman	secretary	dentist
uncle ✓	twelve	father	fifteen	twenty
nine ✓	eight	farmer	engineer	eleven
teacher ✓				

FAMILY

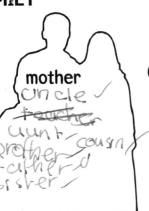

mother
uncle ✓
~~teacher~~
aunt
brother cousin
Father
Sister

NUMBERS

fourteen
nine ✓
twelve
eight
fifteen
twenty
eleven

JOBS

doctor engineer
policeman dentist
farmer
secretary teacher

2 Write the questions and complete the answers.

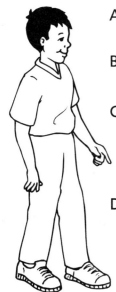

A What's your name? My name is Ramy.

B How old are you ? I'm years old.

C Where dou you live ?

I live near the

D How many have you got brother and sister ?

I've got a 2 sisters and

1 brothers.

3 Look, read and write the names and addresses.

A 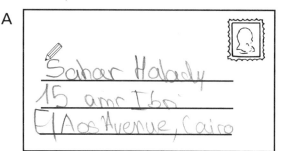   B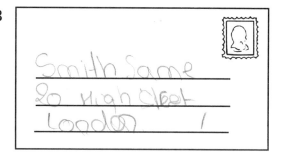

A

Her first name is Sahar. Her family name is El Halaby. Her address is 15 Amr Ibn El Aas Avenue, Cairo.

B

His family name is Smith. His first name is Sam. His address is 20 High Street, London.

4 Read, match and write the numbers on the cars.

Number fifteen, then number twelve, number six, number seventeen, number twenty, number ten and number nine.

5 Time to write the dialogue for the pictures.

A: **Amira, do you like these gold rings?**

B: *they're ok, but look at those necklace*

C: *Yes, they're very nice. I like this one*

D: *I like the handbag*

E: *But this handbag is lovely*

I like that handbag. ✓   They're OK, but look at those necklaces.
Amira, do you like these gold rings? ✔
Yes, they're very nice. I like this one.   But this handbag is lovely. ✓

---

6 Complete the questions and choose your own answers.

Yes, I do. It's/They're very nice/pretty/lovely.
No, I don't.

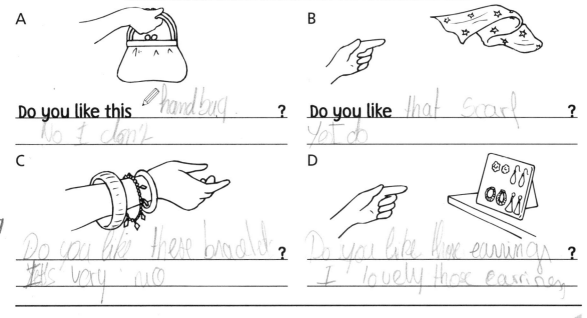

A: **Do you like this** *handbag* ?
No I don't

B: **Do you like** *that scarf* ?
yes I do

C: *Do you like these bracelet* ?
It's very nice

D: *Do you like those earrings* ?
I lovely those earrings

The homework club

1 Time to find the sentences and write.

A

He likes Maths, but his favourite subject is English

C

He likes science but his favourite subject is arabic

B

She likes general knowledge but her favourite subject is religion

D

she likes English, but her favourite subject is sport

She likes English
She likes General Knowledge
He likes Maths
He likes Science

but her favourite subject is Religion.
but English is his favourite subject.
but his favourite subject is Arabic.
but Sports is her favourite subject.

2 Complete and match the questions and answers.

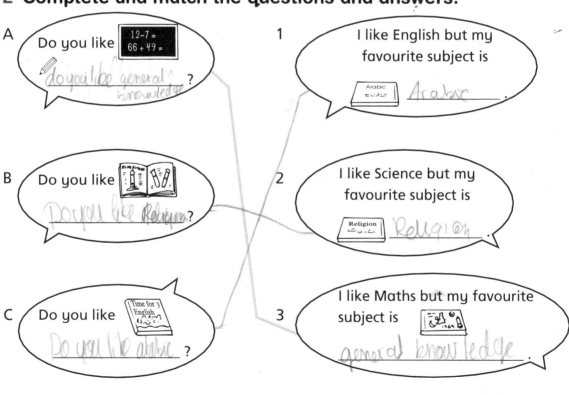

A Do you like
12-7 =
66 + 49 =
do you like general knowledge ?

1 I like English but my favourite subject is
Arabic
Arabic .

B Do you like
Do you like Religion ?

2 I like Science but my favourite subject is
Religion
Religion .

C Do you like
Time for English
Do you like arabic ?

3 I like Maths but my favourite subject is
general knowledge .

3 Read and tick the correct subject.

Look at page 21 in the Pupil's Book.

A Karim likes Maths ☐ but he doesn't like Arabic. ☐
Sports ☒ Science. ☒

B Amin likes Arabic ☒ but he doesn't like Science. ☐
Sports ☐ Sports. ☒

C Farid likes English ☐ but he doesn't like General Knowledge. ☒
Religion ☒ Maths. ☐

D Magda likes Religion ☐ but she doesn't like Science. ☒
Maths ☒ Sports. ☐

E Peter likes Science ☒ but he doesn't like English ☐
Arabic ☐ General Knowledge. ☒

4 Time to circle and correct the mistakes.

Look at page 21 in the Pupil's Book.

Jack doesn't like Maths but he likes Sports. Mahmoud
likes Religion but he doesn't like Science. Omar likes
English but he doesn't like General Knowledge. Khaled
likes Maths but he doesn't like Arabic.

Jack doesn't like Maths but he likes Sports.
Mahmoud likes religion but he doesn't like Science.
Omar likes English but he doesn't

5 Read the grid and write true sentences.

	✔	✘	❤❤❤
Salwa	Maths	Science	Arabic
Susan	General Knowledge	Sports	Religion
Ashraf	English	Maths	Sports
Mohammed	Arabic	General Knowledge	English

<u>Salwa likes Maths but she doesn't like Science. Her favourite subject is Arabic.</u>

Suzan likes General knowledge but she don't like sport
her faourite subject is religion
ashraf likes English but he don't like Maths, his favourite subject is sport
Muhammed He likes Arabic but he don't like general Knowledge
his favourite subject is English

6 Time to find the question and answer.

> you like Do English?

> favourite but is Science. my Yes, subject

Unit 6 At the weekend

---

1 Time to read and match.

A 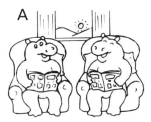 B  C  D

What do you do at the weekend?

1 In the evening, I watch TV. C

2 In the afternoon, we do some homework. B

3 In the morning, we read comics. A

4 In the evening, I help Mum. D

---

2 Find out about your friends and write.

What do you do on Saturday?

In the morning, I help Mum.

	In the morning,	In the afternoon,	In the evening,
Friend 1	I help Mum.	I go to the Mosque	I sleep.
Friend 2	I do some homework	I sleep	I watch TV

Now write and draw what you do on Saturday.

In the morning, I _____

In the afternoon, I _____

In the evening, I _____

● **3 Time to read and complete.**

| sports club | visits her friends | computer games | helps her dad |

On Saturday, Tamara plays _computer games_ in the morning.
Then she goes to the _sport club._ . In the afternoon, she
helps dad . In the evening, she _visits her friends_ .

● **4 Circle the mistakes and write true sentences.**

Look at page 25 of
the Pupil's Book.

On Monday, Karim watches videos. On Tuesday, Karim visits his uncle.
On Wednesday, he reads comics. On Thursday, he plays football. On
Friday, he goes to the sports club.

_On Monday, Karim does some homework. On tuesday,
Karim visits his friends. On wednesday, he reads a book.
On Thursday he plays football. On Friday he
goes to the mosque._

22 Unit 6

5 Who is it? Read and write the name in a sentence.

Look at page 26 of the Pupil's Book.

A   In the morning, I help my dad and I play football.

  In the morning, Jack helps his dad and plays football.

B   On Sunday, I visit my friends and I do some homework.

  On Sunday, she visites her friends and she do some homework.

C   On Friday, I go to the mosque.

  On Friday I go to the mosque

D   In the afternoon, I watch videos.

  In the afternoon, I watch videos

6 Tch or ch ? Write the correct letters.

tch

ch ips

tea___er

wa tch

ch

Unit 7 Taxis, bikes and cars

● 1 **Time to read and match.**

On Monday, I go to school by car.
On Tuesday, I go to school by bus.
On Wednesday, I go to school by taxi.
On Thursday, I go to school on foot.
On Sunday, I go to school by rocket!

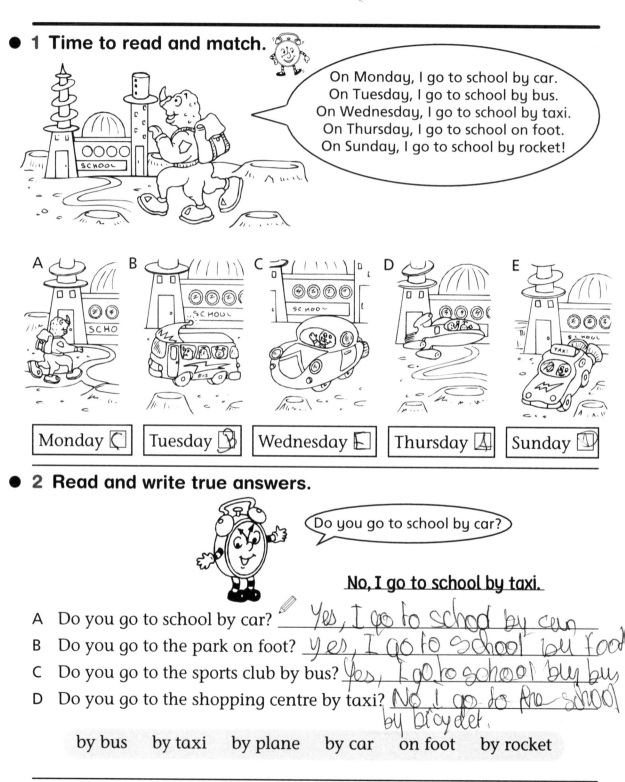

| Monday C | Tuesday B | Wednesday E | Thursday A | Sunday D |

● 2 **Read and write true answers.**

Do you go to school by car?

__No, I go to school by taxi.__

A Do you go to school by car? _Yes, I go to school by car_

B Do you go to the park on foot? _Yes, I go to school by foot_

C Do you go to the sports club by bus? _Yes, I go to school by bus_

D Do you go to the shopping centre by taxi? _No, I go to the school by bicycle._

by bus   by taxi   by plane   by car   on foot   by rocket

● **3 Ask 3 friends and write sentences.**

How do you go to school?

By taxi.

A $\underline{}$ **goes to school** $\underline{}$

B $\underline{}$

C $\underline{}$

● **4 Read and answer the questions.**

Nada   Adam

Adam goes to school by bike, but he goes to the park by bus. His sister, Nada, goes to school on foot. She goes to the park by car. Nada and Adam go to the sports club by taxi.

A Does Adam go to school by car? **No, he doesn't. He** goes to the bike

B Does he go to the park by bike? No, he doesn't. He goes to the bus.

C Does Nada go to school on foot? Yes, she does

D Does she go to the sports club by car? No she doesn't, she go to the by taxi

E Does Adam go to the sports club by taxi? Yes, he does

Unit 7 25

● 5 Time to write the questions.

A

Does he go to the chess club by rocket?

Yes, he goes to the chess club by rocket.

B

'Does she go the school on foot' ?

No, she doesn't. She goes to the chess club by taxi.

C

Does she go to the mosque by taxi ?

Yes, he goes to the mosque by taxi.

D

Does she go to the mosque by car ?

No, she doesn't. She goes to school by bus.

● 6 Use the letters to make 6 kinds of transport.

R O E O C T O A N P L E X I T A C A S B U F T R K

1 ___Rocket___   2 ___taxi___   3 ___bus___

4 ___car___   5 ___Foot___   6 _____

Revision

● **1 Look and write what they are saying.**

I like Maths but my favourite subject is Science!

A

she likes tenis but she favourite subject is English

B

he likes arabic but his favourite subject is tenis

C

she likes general knowledge. but my favoue subject is Maths

D

he likes tenis but my favourite subjects is religion.

● **2 Time to complete the sentences.**

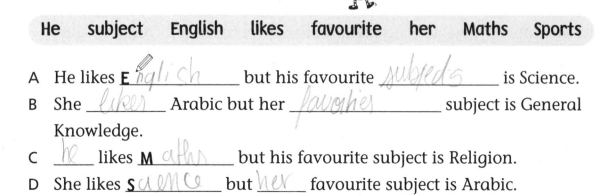

| He | subject | English | likes | favourite | her | Maths | Sports |

A He likes E nglish _____ but his favourite subjects _____ is Science.

B She _ likes _ Arabic but her _ favories _ subject is General Knowledge.

C _ he _ likes M aths _____ but his favourite subject is Religion.

D She likes S ience _____ but her _____ favourite subject is Arabic.

3 Write 4 true sentences.

				sports club.
				mosque.
	Monday		go to the	comics.
	Tuesday		read	a book.
	Wednesday		watch	TV.
On	Thursday	I	visit	videos.
	Friday	we	help	my friends.
	Saturday		do	my cousins.
	Sunday		play	my mum.
				my dad.
				some homework.
				football.

_____

_____

_____

_____

4 Read and tick the correct description.

Saturday

Sunday

A On Saturday, we go to the shopping centre in the morning. In the afternoon, we go to the sports club. In the evening, we play computer games. On Sunday, we help Mum in the morning. In the afternoon, we read comics and watch TV. In the evening, we do some homework. ☐

B On Saturday, we go to the shopping centre in the morning. In the afternoon, we go to the sports club. In the evening, we play computer games. On Sunday, we help Mum in the morning. In the afternoon, we do some homework. In the evening, we read comics and watch TV. ☐

5 Time to read and write.

A

We don't go to school by bus,
we go by taxi.

B

C

D

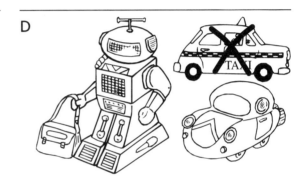

6 Read and answer the questions.

A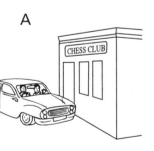

Omar

B

Sahar

C

Nasser

D

Faisal

A   Does Omar go to the chess club on foot?   **No, he doesn't.**

B   Does Sahar go to school by taxi?

C   Does Nasser go to the sports club by bus?

D   Does Faisal go to the mosque by bike?

Unit 9 What's the weather like?

● **1 Time to look and write.**

It's hot. It's quite cold. It's cold. It's quite hot. It's very cold. It's very hot.

← 40 degrees _It's very hote_

← 35 degrees _it's hot_

← 30 degrees _it's quite hot_

← 15 degrees _it's quite cold_

← 10 degrees _It's cold_

← 5 degrees _it's very cold_

● **2 Match and write.**

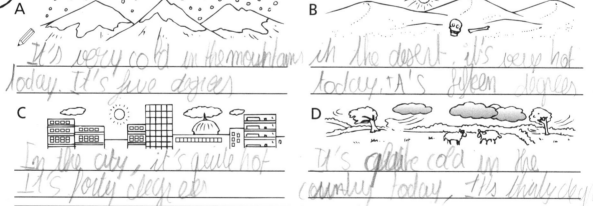

A _It's very cold in the mountains today. It's five degrees_

B _in the desert, it's very hot today. It's fifteen degrees_

C _In the city, it's quite hot. It's forty degrees_

D _It's quite cold in the country today. It's thirty degrees_

It's very cold in the mountains today.	It's forty degrees.
In the city, it's quite hot.	It's fifteen degrees.
In the desert, it's very hot today.	It's five degrees.
It's quite cold in the country today.	It's thirty degrees.

3 Time to fill in the missing months.

December August May September February April July October

January	*February*	March	*April*
May	June	*July*	*August*
September	*october*	November	*december*

4 Draw and write the seasons and months in your country.

spring ✔
summer
autumn
winter

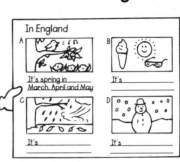

In England

A

It's spring in
March, April and May

B

It's

C

It's

D

It's

A

__In my country, it's spring in__ *June*
July august

B

__In my country, it's__ *summer in*
june july august

C

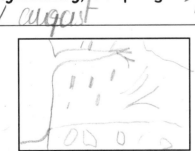

__In my country, it's__ *autumn in*
semptember, october, november

D

__In my country, it's__ *winter in*
january, february, march, April, May
december

● 5 Read and complete the grid.

In the desert today, it's very hot. It's 40 degrees. In the city it's 35 degrees, so it's hot. It's 30 degrees and quite hot in the country today. But in the mountains, it's only 15 degrees. It's quite cold.

	degrees	weather
city	35	it's hot
country	30	it's quite hot
desert	40	it's very hot
mountains	15	it's quite cold

● 6 Read and write about the weather today.

I live in the city. It's spring. It's May. It's 30 degrees today. It's quite hot.

I live in the city, it's spring. It's April. It's 30 degrees today. It's quite hot.

Unit 10 Who's at the club?

1 Read and answer the questions.

A Who's watching a video? *Amira's watching a video*
B Who's painting a picture? *reem's painting a picture*
C Who's making a puppet? *noha's making a puppet*
D Who's making a drink? *susy's making a drink*

2 Choose 4 children and write sentences about them.

Amir's watching a video. *Adel's reading a comic.* *You*
Youssef's painting a picture. Munir's writing a story
Jack's making a puppet. Mark's building a house.
Karim's playing a game

3 Time to write the questions.

A   B   C   D   E   F   G   H

1   **Is A riding a bike?**   Yes, he's riding a bike.

2   *they're B and building a house* ?   Yes, they're building a house.

3   *the D, watching tv* ?   Yes, he's watching a video.

4   *they E and F building puppets* ?   Yes, they're making a puppet.

5   *C and H sleeping* ?   No, they're sleeping.

4 Write the answers.

A   Is Jack making a puppet?
No, he isn't making a puppet.
He's watching a video.

B   Is Amira writing a story?
No, she isn't writing a story
she's making a drink

C   Is Alex making a drink?
No, he isn't making a drink
He's making a puppet

D   Are Noha and Suzy painting a picture?
No, they're painting a picture
they are building a house

● **5 Read and tick the correct description.**

A
Jack's painting a picture, Suzy's making a puppet, Alex is playing a game. Mum's making a drink and Dad's building a house. ☐

B
Jack's painting a picture, Suzy's making a puppet, Alex is building a house. Mum's making a drink and Dad's watching TV. ☒

C
Jack's painting a picture, Suzy's making a puppet, Alex is building a house. Mum's watching TV and Dad's making a drink. ☐

● **6 Circle the mistakes and write true sentences.**

A
Karim isn't making a puppet.
He's making a drink.

B
Jack isn't watching TV.
He's building a house.

C
Noha isn't painting a picture.
She's reading a comic.

D
Suzy isn't watching TV.
She's building a house.

A   Karim isn't making a drink. He's making a puppet
B   Jack isn't building a house he's watching tv
C   Noha isn't reading a story she's painting a picture
D   Suzy isn't watching Tv she's making a drink

Unit 11 At the sports club

● **1 Time to read and write the name.**

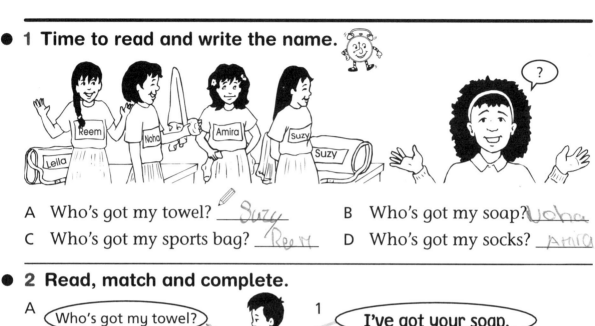

A   Who's got my towel? _Suzy_   B   Who's got my soap? _Noha_
C   Who's got my sports bag? _Reem_   D   Who's got my socks? _Amira_

● **2 Read, match and complete.**

A   Who's got my towel?

1   **I've got your soap.**

B   Who's got my football boots?

2   _I've got your towel_

C   Who's got my soap?

3   _I've got your shoes_

D   Who's got my sports bag?

4   _I've got your sport bag_

E   Who's got my socks?

5   _I've got your football boot_

3 Time to read and complete.

We've got our ✏️ _pen_ , our _book_ and our _bag_ , but we haven't got our _drink_ and we haven't got our _penals_.

4 Write what they're saying.

Who's got their drinks, their books, their pencils and their bags?

A   We've got our ✏️ _penals , our bouks and our bags_

B   _We've got our drinks, our penals ans our bags._

C   _we've got our bags, our books and our drinks_

5 Circle the mistakes and write correct sentences.

A

> We've got our football boots and our socks, but we haven't got our sports bags.

We've got our socks and our sport bags
but we haven't got our football boots

B

> We've got our pencils and our books, but we haven't got our drinks.

We've got our drinks and our pencils
but we haven't got our books

C

> We've got our socks and our soap, but we haven't got our football boots.

We've got our football boots and soap
but we haven't got our socks

6 Time to read, write and match.

A [2]   B [3]   C [1]

1 We earrings. got our haven't   We haven't got our earrings

2 my got Who's bike?   Who's got my bike

3 boots. I got my football haven't   I haven't got my football boots

Unit 12 Revision

● **1 Time to sort and write.**

building, writing, January, summer, winter, making, October, playing, spring, June, May, December, painting, autumn

MONTHS	SEASONS	ACTIONS
January	winter	building
May	spring	making
June	summer	painting
October	spring	playing
December		writing

● **2 Write sentences.**

What's the weather like today?

	degrees	weather
desert	40	very hot
city	10	cold
country	30	quite hot
mountains	5	very cold

A In the desert, it's 40 degrees. It's very hot.

B In the city, It's 10 degrees It's cold

C In the country, It's 30 degrees It's quite hot

D In the mountains, It's 5 degrees. It's very cold

3 Circle the mistakes and write true sentences.

Amira's playing a game and Reem's watching a video. Suzy's making a puppet and Noha's writing a story. Dina's building a house and Mum's making a drink.

Amira's watching a video. Suzy's making a puppet and Noha's building a house. Dina's making a drink, Reem's writing a story and Mum's painting a picture

4 Time to complete the dialogue.

Adel: ___Is___ Jack making a puppet?

Munir: No, _he isn't making a puppet_ He's _painting a picture_ .

Adel: Is Mark painting a picture?

Munir: No, Mark isn't painting a picture. He's _making a puppet_ .

Adel: Who's reading a comic?

Munir: Karim's _reading a comic_ .

Adel: Are Walid and Youssef playing a game?

Munir: Yes, they're _playing a game_ .

5 Match the bubble to the person.

1 I've got your drink!

2 Who's got my drink!

3 I've got my pen and pencil, but I haven't got my book.

4 We've got our pencils and our books, but we haven't got our pens.

5 Who's got their pens, their pencils and their books?

6 Put in capital letters and full stops.

Put capital letters for months, for names, and at the beginning of a sentence. Put full stops at the end of a sentence. Like this:

In May, Leila visits her cousins.

A noha is watching a video

Noha is watching a video

B it's very hot in the desert in august

It's very hot in the desert in August

C it's quite cold in the mountains in winter

It's quite cold in the mountain inwnter

Unit 13 — What are you going to do today?

● 1 Time to look and write.

What are you going to do today?

I'm going to visit my aunt.

cook lunch ✔
visit my aunt ✔
watch a video ✔
buy some food

A *Jack:* he's going to visite her aunt
B *Mum:* she's going cook lunch
C *Alex:* he's going watch a video

● 2 Ask 3 friends and write.

What are you going to do today?

Friend 1	I'm going to watch a video
Friend 2	I'm going to visit my aunt
Friend 3	I'm going to play football

3 Tick the correct box.

A

Suzy's going to   buy some food. ☐
           visit Aunt Jane. ☑

B

Karim's going to   watch TV. ☐
           watch a video. ☑

C

Reem's going to   visit Uncle Zaki. ☐
           the sports club. ☑

D

Noha's going to   cook lunch. ☐
           buy some food. ☑

4 Time to complete the sentences.

man   men   woman   women

A

The man is going to visit his
uncle

B

The women is going
to buy some food

C

The men are going to
watch tv

D

The women is going
to cook lunch

5 Read and answer the questions.

A

What is Jack going to do?

He's going to watch _tv_

B

What is Alex going to do?

he's going do visit her a

C

What is Amira going to do?

She's _going to cook lunch_

D

What is Dina going to do?

She's going to buy some fo

6 What are you going to do at the weekend?

At the weekend I going to the mosque fo

Unit 14 Our school uniform

● **1 Time to read, find and complete.**

● = blue   ▲ = white   ■ = black

MODEL SCHOOL

Mr Moussa

Our school is ‟Model‟ School Our teacher is Mr Moussa . Our shirts
are blue , our short are black, our socks are white and our
shoes are black .

● **2 Write sentences about your school.**

Our school is . . .   Our school uniform is . . .
Our teacher is . . .   Our shirts/shorts/skirts/socks/shoes are . . .

Our school is modern school
Our school uniform is a dress
our teacher is Mr Lusterholtz
our dress are pink jolly shoes are
furniture

● **3 Write the questions then colour the clowns.**

A

What's color are their?

Their hats are red.

B

What's color are theirsuit?

Their suits are yellow.

C

What's color are their shoe ?

Their shoes are blue.

D

what's color are their socks ?

Their socks are green.

● **4 Colour the clowns and write the answers.**

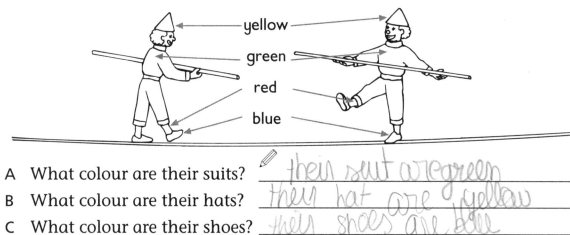

yellow
green
red
blue

A What colour are their suits? their suit are green

B What colour are their hats? their hat are yellow

C What colour are their shoes? their shoes are blue

D What colour are their socks? their socks are red

5 Circle the mistakes and write true sentences.

Our bikes are white, our car is black, our cats are grey. Our skirts are grey, our shirts are white, our socks are white and our shoes are black.

Our bikes are black, our car is white, our cat are grey. Our skirt are black, our socks are grey and our shoes are black

6 Write a question and an answer and colour the suits.

colour their are suits? What

What colour are their suit

and suits Their red. blue are

Their suits are blue and red.

Unit 15 City and country

● **1 Read and tick the correct sentence.**

A

In the country it's noisy. ☐

In the city it's noisy. ☑

B

In the city the roads are narrow. ☐

In the country the roads are narrow. ☑

C

In the city it's exciting! ☑

In the country it's exciting! ☐

D

There are busy shops in the country. ☐

There are busy shops in the city. ☑

● **2 Time to read then complete the sentences.**

city   big buildings   exciting!   busy shops   wide streets   city

I live in the 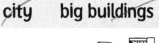 _city_ . In the  _city_ , there are

big building , _busy shops_

and  _wide streets_ . It's _exciting!_

3 Read, match and write the city or the country.

A [2] B [1] C [5]

D [3] E [4]

1   It's quiet. _theCountry_ .
2   There are big buildings. _the city_ .
3   There are lots of fields. _the country_ .
4   It's boring! _the city_ .
5   The roads are dangerous. _the city_ .

4 Read, match, then write the answers.

A Where do you live? — _I live in the country_

B Is it quiet or noisy? — _quiet_

C Are there any fields? — _Yes, there are lot of fields_

D Are there any animals? — _Yes, there are cows and goats_

1   It's quiet.
2   Yes, there are cows and goats.
3   I live in the country.
4   Yes, there are a lot of fields.

5 Read and tick the correct picture.

A ☑

B ☐

It's quiet.   There are a lot of fields.   There are goats, cows and sheep.
The roads are narrow.

6 Time to write about where you live.

<u>I live in</u> Theaty, There are a busy shop.
There are big beulding and a dangerou
roads

Unit 16 Revision

● **1 Time to sort and write.**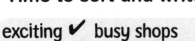

exciting ✔	busy shops	skirts	noisy	dangerous	shorts
shirts	big buildings	shoes	socks	narrow roads	quiet
boring	cows and sheep	fields	goats	wide streets	hats

CLOTHES   **CITY**   **COUNTRY**

shirt
skirts
shoes
socks
shorts
hats

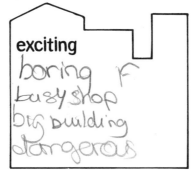

exciting
boring
busy shop
big building
dangerous

cows
and sheep
fields
goats
wide streets

● **2 Read, match and write men or women.**

A

B

C

D

1 The _____men_____ are going to watch a video.
2 The _____women_____ are going to visit my aunt.
3 The _____women_____ are going to cook lunch.
4 The _____men_____ are going to buy some food.

● **3 Time to read and colour.**

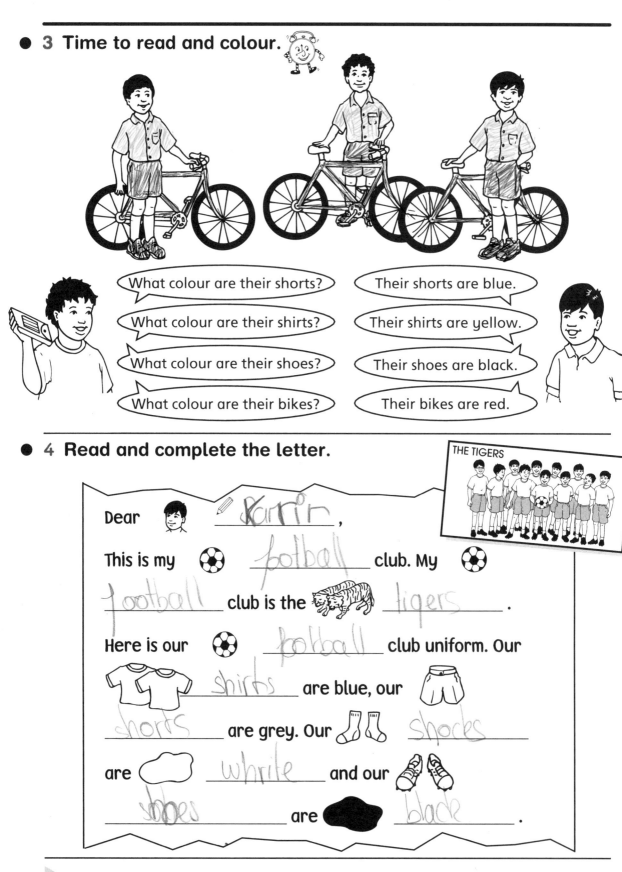

What colour are their shorts? — Their shorts are blue.

What colour are their shirts? — Their shirts are yellow.

What colour are their shoes? — Their shoes are black.

What colour are their bikes? — Their bikes are red.

● **4 Read and complete the letter.**

THE TIGERS

Dear ___Karrin___ ,

This is my ⚽ ___fotball___ club. My ⚽

___football___ club is the 🐯 ___tigers___ .

Here is our ⚽ ___fotball___ club uniform. Our

___shirts___ are blue, our

___shorts___ are grey. Our 🧦 ___shoces___

are ___white___ and our 👟

___shoes___ are ___black___ .

● **5 Time to find the word.**

1   2   3

4   5   6

7   8

1	b	i	k	e
2	s	o	f	t
3	s	h	i	r	t
4	f	i	e	l	d
5	v	i	d	e	o
6	s	k	i	r	t
7	c	o	u	n	t	r	y
8	g	o	a	t

The new word is ____building____ .

● **6 Read, choose and write the correct answers.**

Karim: Do you like where you live, Aunt Zeinab?

Aunt Zeinab: _Yes, there are a lot of fields near my_

Karim: Is it quiet or noisy?

Aunt Zeinab: _It's quiet_

Karim: Are there any animals?

Aunt Zeinab: _Yes, there are cows, sheep and goats_

Karim: But is it boring?

Aunt Zeinab: _No, it's exciting_

    A   No, it's exciting!
    B   It's quiet.
    C   Yes, there are a lot of fields near my house.
    D   Yes, there are cows, sheep and goats.

Unit 17 What's his job?

● **1 Read and write the place.**

shop   library   hospital   bank

A A librarian works in a   library

B A nurse works in a      hospital

C A bank clerk works in a      bank

D A shop assistant works in a      shop

● **2 Read and answer the questions.**

A    B    C    D

A Does she work in a bank?   <u>No, she doesn't.</u>
B Does he work in a hospital?   No, he doesn't
C Does she work in a bank?   Yes, she does
D Does he work in a library?   Yes, he does

3 Follow the lines and answer the question.

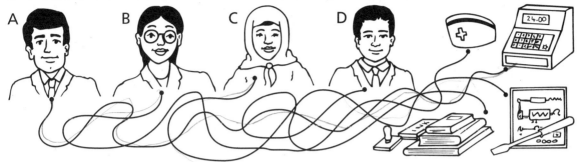

A   What's his job?   **He's a** shop assistant

B   What's her job?   **She's a** librarian

C   What's her job?   she's a engineer

D   What's his job?   he's a nurse

engineer
librarian
nurse
shop assistant

4 Time to fill the gaps.

A   **What's her job?**   She's a nurse.

B   What's her job?   She's a bank clerk.

C   What's his job?   **He's a** shop assistant

D   What's his job?   He's a librarian

● **5 Time to write the answers.**

A Does she work in a hospital?

  No, she doesn't. She's a secretary.

B Does she work in a shop?

  No, she doesn't she's a nurse

C Does he work in a school?

  No, he doesn't, he's a librarian

D  Does she work in a school?

  Yes, she's a teacher

E  Does he work in a hospital?

  No, he doesn't, he's a policeman

● **6 Read and write in the jobs.**

Person	Job
Andrew	shop assistant
Mariam	nurse
Khaled	librarian
Amna	bank clerk

Andrew doesn't work in a bank, a library or a hospital.
Mariam doesn't work in a bank, a library or a shop.
Khaled doesn't work in a bank, a shop or a hospital.
Amna doesn't work in a hospital, a shop or a library.

library
bank
hospital
shop ✔

Unit 18 What's the matter?

● **1 Time to read and complete.** stomach   back   throat   tooth

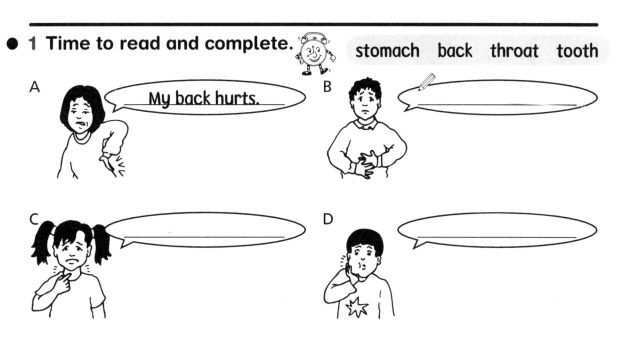

A — My back hurts.

B

C

D

● **2 Write the names then answer the question.**

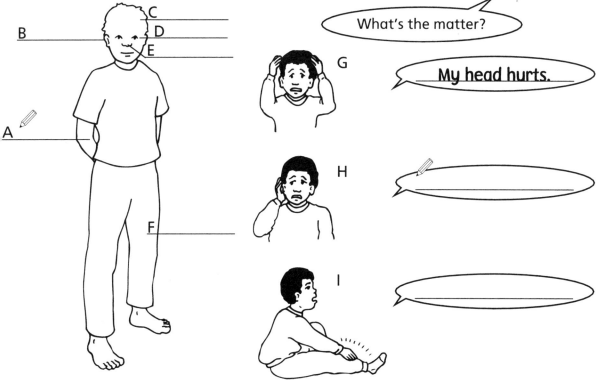

What's the matter?

G — My head hurts.

H

I

3 Read and match.

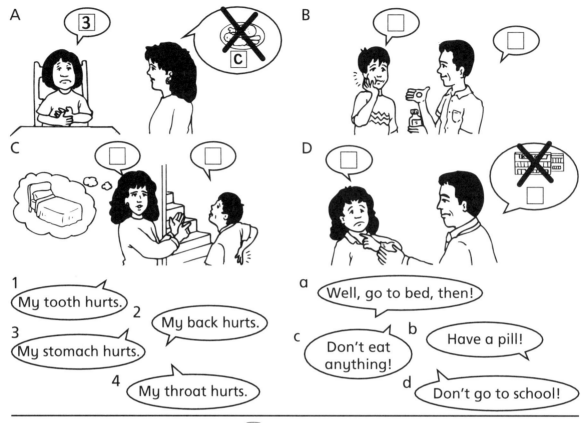

1 My tooth hurts.
2 My back hurts.
3 My stomach hurts.
4 My throat hurts.

a Well, go to bed, then!
b Have a pill!
c Don't eat anything!
d Don't go to school!

4 Time to look and write.

A Don't _____

B _____

C _____

D _____

5 Read and circle the mistakes.

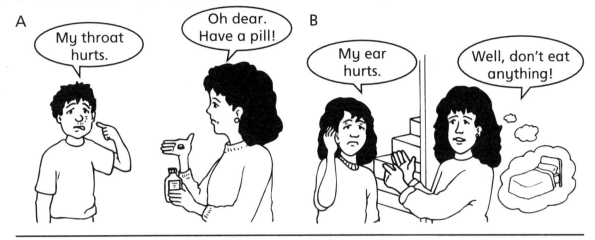

6 Time to fill the gaps.

hurts   eat   leg   school   pill   head   bed   eye

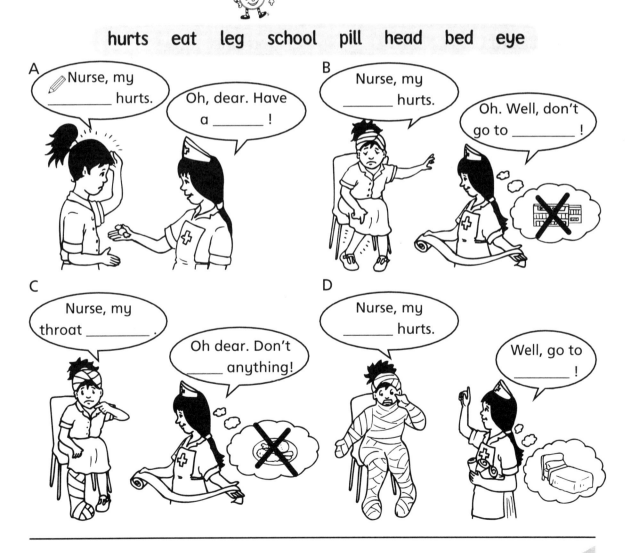

You must revise!

1 Read and tick T (true) or F (false).

		T	F
A	You must revise for an hour every day.	☐	☐
B	You must read comics.	☐	☐
C	You mustn't go to the library.	☐	☐
D	You mustn't go to bed early.	☐	☐
E	You mustn't watch TV.	☐	☐

2 Time to read and complete.

A

You mustn't _____

B

You must _____

C

You _____

D

You _____

3 Circle and correct the mistakes.

> You must read comics!
> You mustn't go to the library!
> You must revise for an hour every day!
> You mustn't go to bed early!
> You must feed your cat every day!
> You mustn't share your sweets!

4 Read and write sentences.

A | share/sweets ✔

I must share my sweets.

B | play/matches ✘

C | fight/class ✘

D | read/comics ✘

E | library/every day ✔

● 5 Look and write sentences.

A

You mustn't play in the road.

B

C

D
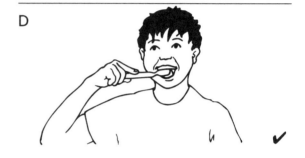

E

F

● 6 Time to find the sentence.

Y   m   f   y   c   e   d

Unit 20 Revision

● **1 Sort and write.**

stomach ✔	throat	tooth	shop assistant	nose	bank clerk
teacher	school	nurse	library	bank	hospital
engineer	shop	back	dentist	ear	eye

PARTS OF THE BODY

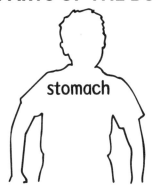

stomach

JOBS

PLACES

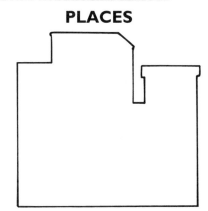

● **2 Time to read and match.**

A  Does she work in a library?

1 No, he doesn't. He's a bank clerk.

B  Does he work in a school?

2 No, she doesn't. She's a teacher.

C Does she work in a bank?

3 She's a librarian.

D  What's her job?

4 No, she doesn't. She's a nurse.

3 Read and fill the gaps.

Jack: Mum, my _____ hurts.

Mum: Well, go to _____ and _____ !

Alex: My _____ hurts.

Mum: Here, have a _____ !

Suzy: Mum, my _____ hurts!

Mum: Well, _____ !

Suzy: Hurray!

4 Time to read and draw.

A

My stomach hurts.

B

My leg hurts.

C

My nose hurts.

D

My throat hurts.

5 Read, match and write.

A

_____

_____

B

_____

_____

C

_____

_____

D

_____

_____

You must	fight in class.
You mustn't	share your sweets.
You mustn't	feed your cat every day.
You must	read comics in class.

6 Time to read and write.

I've got a test next week. I must revise for an hour every day. I must go to the library every day. I mustn't watch videos and I mustn't read comics. I must go to bed early.

Things to do for test:

1 I must _____

2 _____

3 _____

4 I mustn't _____

5 _____

Unit 21 When is it on?

● **1 Time to read and match.**

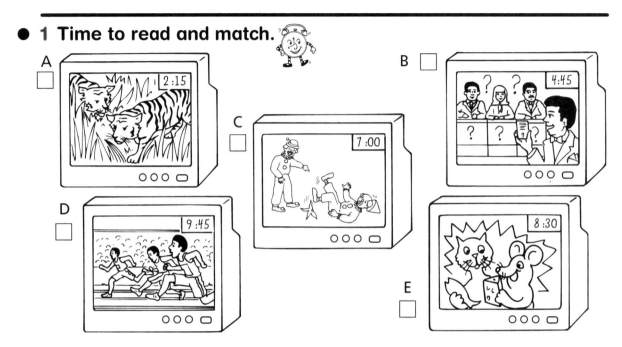

1 The cartoon show is on. It's half past eight.
2 And now it's the wildlife programme at quarter past two.
3 It's quarter to ten. It's time for the sports programme.
4 It's quarter to five. The quiz show is on.
5 It's seven o'clock. It's the comedy show!

● **2 Read and answer the questions. Look at exercise 1.**

A When is the cartoon show on?

__It's on at__

B When is the wildlife programme on?

C When is the quiz show on?

D When is the comedy show on?

E When is the sports programme on?

3 Write the questions and complete the answers.

Cartoon Fun	.... 4.00
Wildlife on 3	.... 5.30
Sports Today	.... 7.45
Quiz Time	.... 6.15

A

What's your favourite programme?

It's the sports programme.

When is it on?

It's on at quarter to eight.

B

_____ ?

It's the wildlife programme.

_____ ?

It's on at half past five.

C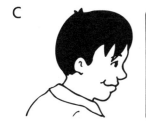

_____ ?

It's the _____

_____

It's on at quarter past six.

D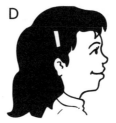

_____ ?

It's the cartoon show.

_____ ?

_____

4 Ask 3 friends and fill the grid.

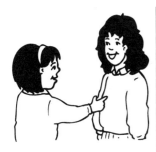

	Favourite programme	Time
Friend 1		
Friend 2		
Friend 3		

5 Read and write the programme.

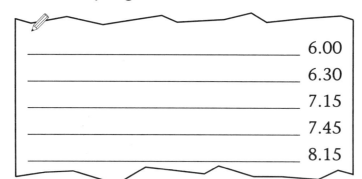

_____	6.00
_____	6.30
_____	7.15
_____	7.45
_____	8.15

Cartoons on One is on at six o'clock. Next, it's *Quiz Time. Quiz Time* is on at half past six. *Wildlife Camera* is on at quarter past seven. Then, at quarter to eight, it's *Sports Sports Sports*, and *Comedy For You* is on at quarter past eight.

6 Time to find and write.

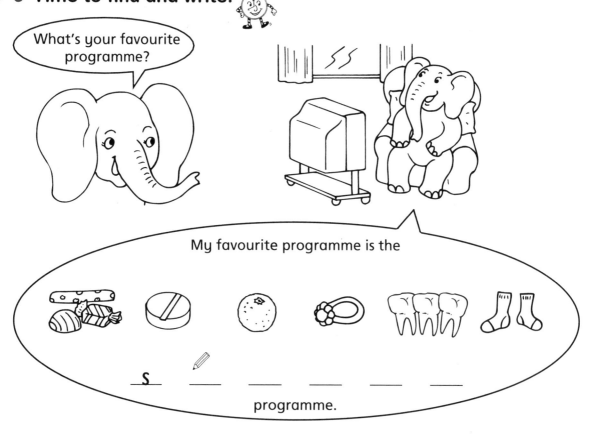

What's your favourite programme?

My favourite programme is the

_S_ _ _ _ _ _ _

programme.

Unit 22 In the school library

1 Time to write the answers.

Yes, there is. Here's one.
No, there isn't.

A Is there a book about the pyramids?

B Is there a book about sport?

C Is there a book about history?

D Is there a book about animals?

2 Write the questions.

A Is there a book about animals?

B

C

D

3 Time to read and complete.

A (Are there any oranges?) (Yes, there are some.)

B (Are there ⟋ potatoes?) (No, there aren't any.)

C (Are tomatoes?) (Yes, there)

D (Are olives?) (No,)

4 Circle and correct the mistakes.

A *Reem:* Are there any oranges? ⟋

    Noha: No, there aren't any. _____

B *Amira:* Are there any olives?

    Noha: Yes, there are some. _____

C *Reem:* Are there any tomatoes?

    Noha: Yes, there are some. _____

D *Amira:* Are there any bananas?

    Noha: No, there aren't any. _____

5 Draw a picture of your bedroom and answer the questions.

A Is there a clock? _____

B Are there any toys? _____

C Is there a book about animals? _____

D Is there a TV? _____

E Are there any comics? _____

F Is there a computer? _____

G Are there any pictures? _____

Unit 23 The end of year display

● **1 Time to read and match.**

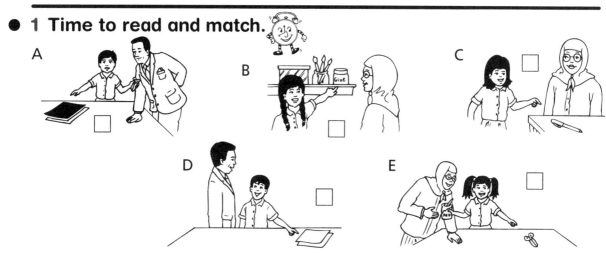

A
B
C
D
E

1   I want the glue, please.
2   I don't want the paint. I want the scissors.
3   I want the white paper.
4   I don't want the scissors, I want the black paper.
5   I want the pen, please.

● **2 Read and complete.**

A   What do _____ ?

B   I want the _____

C   I _____ glue, please.

D   I don't want the black paper. I _____

3 Read and put a tick or a cross.

Khaled wants the scissors, the glue and the white paper. He doesn't want the black paper and he doesn't want the pen.

Ahmed wants the glue, the pen and the black paper. He doesn't want the scissors and he doesn't want the white paper.

Mahmoud doesn't want the scissors and he doesn't want the black paper. He wants the glue, the pen and the white paper.

	scissors	glue	pen	white paper	black paper
Khaled	✔	✔	✘	✔	✘
Ahmed					
Mahmoud					

4 Complete the questions and answers.

A __What does__ __Alex want?__

__He wants the__ __football.__

B _____ __?__

__She wants the__ __scissors.__

C _____ __?__

__He__ _____ __sweets.__

D _____ __?__

__She__ _____ __necklace.__

5 What do they want? Circle and correct the mistakes.

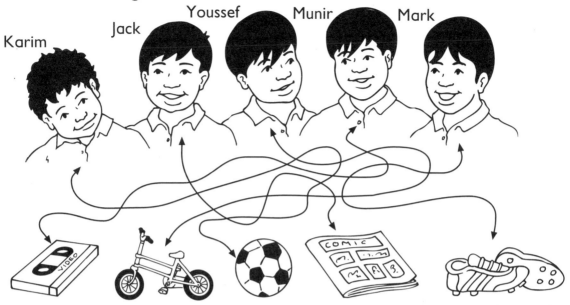

Karim   Jack   Youssef   Munir   Mark

A   Karim wants a football.
B   Jack doesn't want a football. He wants a video.
C   Youssef doesn't want a football. He wants a sports bag.
D   Munir wants a comic.
E   Mark doesn't want football boots. He wants a comic.

B   _Jack doesn't want a video. He wants a comic._

C   _____

D   _____

E   _____

6 Time to write what they're saying.

A   I want some
    sweets.

B   _____

C   _____

Unit 24 Revision

1 Read then number the pictures.

A ☐ B 1 C ☐ D ☐ E ☐

It's Monday.
And first it's *Cartoon Time* at six
o'clock. Then, at half past six, it's *Wildlife Now*.
Next, it's *Quiz Pyramid*. *Quiz Pyramid* is on
at quarter past seven. *Comedy Fun* is on at
eight o'clock, and then it's *Sports Hour*
at half past eight.

2 Look, read and tick the right question.

A Are there any comics? ☐   Yes, there are some.
    footballs? ☐

B Is there a handbag? ☐   Yes, there is one.
    scarf? ☐

C Are there any books? ☐   No, there aren't any.
    comics? ☐

D Are there any shoes? ☐   Yes, there are some.
    football boots? ☐

E Is there a cat? ☐   No, there isn't.
    goat? ☐

3 Choose and draw 4 things from the list.

a book about the pyramids   a TV   a football   a book about sport   a clock   a cat

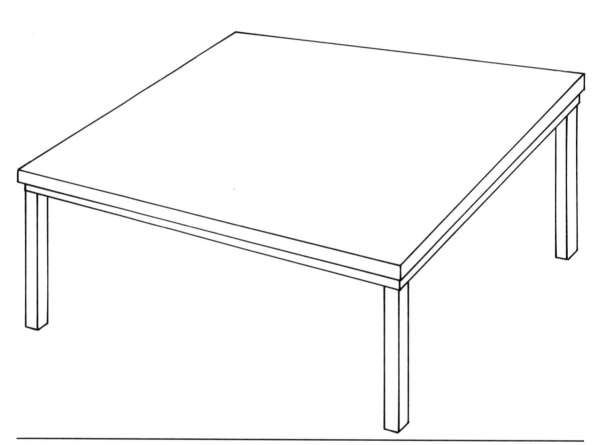

4 Answer Yes, there is. or No, there isn't.

A   Is there a book about the pyramids? _____

B   Is there a book about sport? _____

C   Is there a football? _____

D   Is there a TV? _____

E   Is there a cat? _____

F   Is there a clock? _____

5 Complete the sentences and make a robot.

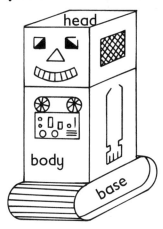

I want some card, some glue, some scissors, some pencils and some paints.

card
paints
glue
scissors
pencils

A

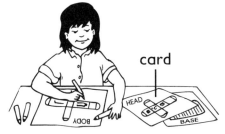

Colour the robot with the _____ or the _____ .

B

Cut out the 3 pieces of the robot with the _____ .

C

Fold the _____ .

D

Glue the robot together with the _____ .

Progress check

● **1 Colour the clown and the ball, then tick the box.**

I have finished Units 1 to 4. ☐

● **2 Colour the clown and the balls, then tick the box.**

I have finished Units 5 to 8. ☐

3 Colour the clown and the balls, then tick the box.

I have finished Units 9 to 12. ☐

4 Colour the clown and the balls, then tick the box.

I have finished Units 13 to 16. ☐

● **5 Colour the clown and the balls, then tick the box.**

I have finished Units 17 to 20. ☒

● **6 Colour the clown and the balls, then tick the box.**

I have finished Units 21 to 24. ☒